Australian Animals

30 Beautiful Animal Pages to Color

Unwind with creatively made coloring pages for stress relief, creativity and fun

14 Peaks

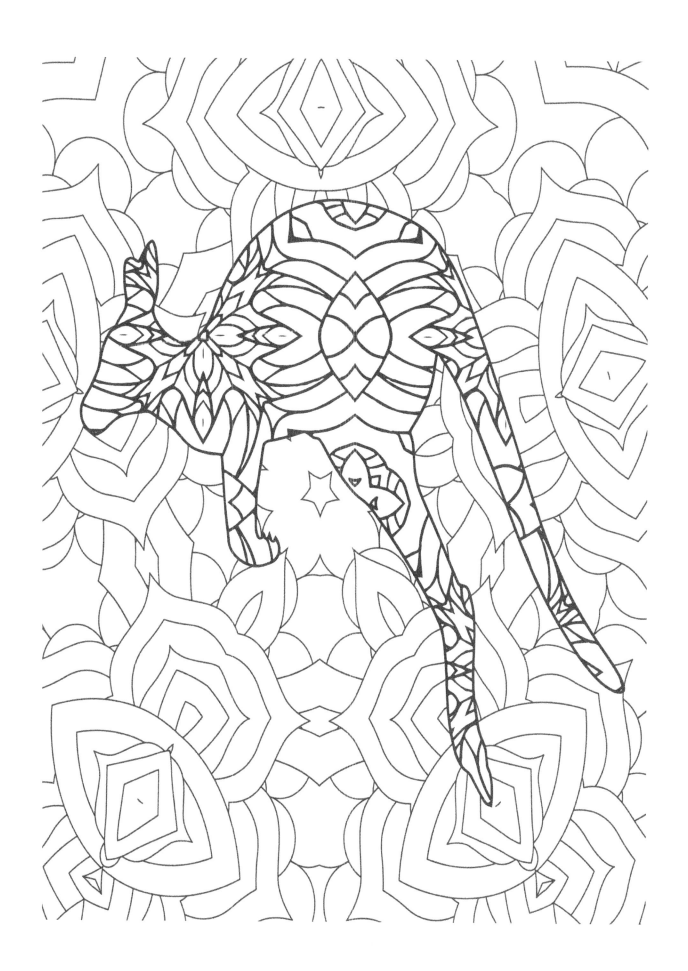

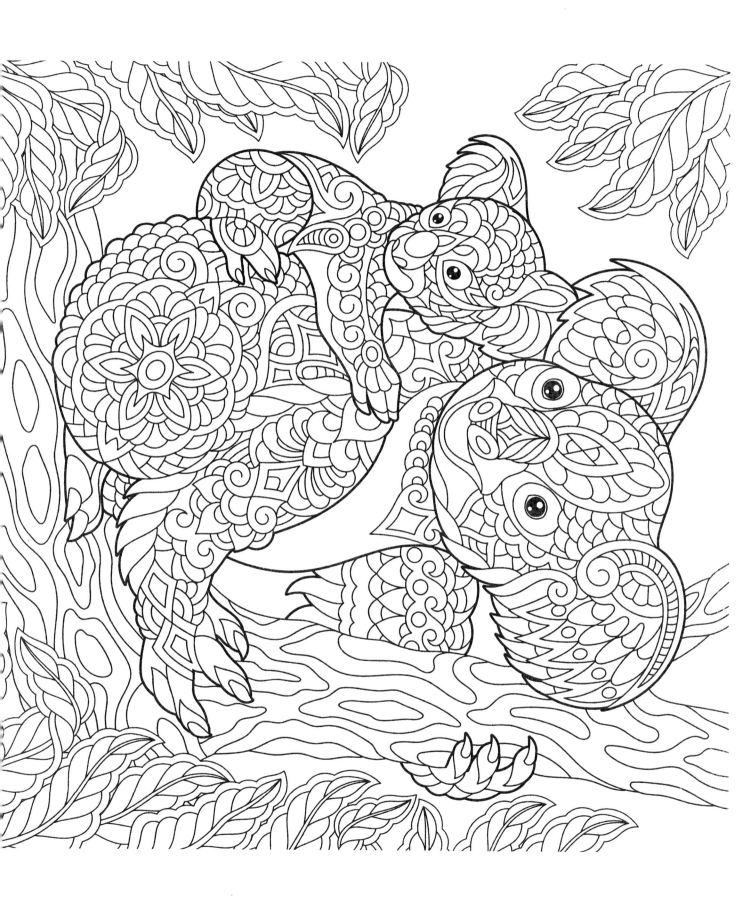

More Coloring Coming to You

We have new books coming out every month and holiday themed books each holiday. Find free printable coloring pages at www.14-peaks.com

About The Author

14 Peaks is a publishing company that was started after the founder finished an extreme race called Primal Quest. After numerous requests for race details, the search for a platform to tell the story began. With the help of the talented CJ Jerabek, the story went to print.

After coaching for 25 years and teaching martial arts for 10, she put together a new kind of team, a publishing team. It takes a great team to help authors showcase their hard work and that is the vision.

"You don't have to be an expert at everything; you just have to bring in those who are."

Wonderful, experts were brought on board that make a strong team. Professionals, who give expertise in their field, making this a winning publishing company.

Made in the USA
Coppell, TX
28 January 2020